Enjoy our...

BIRD DANCE

A Native American Tradition
for all to enjoy

Best Wishes
Deborah Armstrong

Wishing you all
the best,
Eleanor Flores

By Eleanor Flores

Table of Contents

DEDICATION

To:

Leatrice Marie Tourtillott

(1982-2013)

and Melanie Darlene Jose

(1984-2013),

two beautiful cousins

taken together way too soon,

due to a tragic traffic accident,

and two of the best Bird Dancers

on the Quechan Indian Reservation.

*****

INTRODUCTION

Hi! My name is Eleanor Flores, and I am excited to share with you this Native American tradition, known as bird dancing. Please allow me to give you a brief history of how this came about...

I was born and raised in Los Angeles, California, the eldest of nine children. My hard-working Dad, Jerry Flores, retired from CalTrans, after 33 years keeping the freeways safe and clean. My wonderful Mom and Dad were married over 60 years. They nourished us with love and food in our two-bedroom, one-bath home, which the 11 of us enjoyed, until I was 17 years old and left home to live on campus.

Thanks to Jack Wright, my college advisor at Franklin High School, I was awarded a four-year academic scholarship to attend Pepperdine University in Malibu. This is where I met my soulmate, this gorgeous 6'-5" full-blooded Native American, Delmar L. Jose, Jr., who had long thick black hair, and ever so kind. He was the oldest of eight children and was also awarded a four-year academic scholarship.

Delmar was born and raised on the Quechan Indian Reservation, located in Winterhaven, California, which borders Yuma, Arizona. It was such an unforgettable experience for both of us to have spectacular views of the Pacific Ocean from our dorms!

Unfortunately, Delmar had to leave Pepperdine after two years because of a family emergency. So when he asked me to marry him and move to his homeland, without hesitation, I left Pepperdine and my stomping grounds and lived on the reservation with him. It may have been over 115 degrees on many days, surviving with no air conditioning in our home, but we were unbelievably happy together. You just couldn't help but embrace his culture and admire his warmhearted family.

Delmar had told me that many Native Americans who live on the reservation believe that they are all related somehow because back in the day, the settlers changed many of the Native Americans' last names, which made it almost impossible for them to distinguish how each person is related as time passed. This is why Delmar's last name was "Jose." I always felt welcomed living on the reservation because it is truly a tight-knit community of family with open arms.

Sadly, Delmar passed away at age 43, but he left me the peace of knowing the genuine feeling of unconditional love of a soulmate. Almost all of Delmar's family still live on the reservation, and I always enjoy visiting them. They love to laugh. I kick dirt on the res whenever I can, which grounds me from the hustle of living in a big city.

Recently, as one of Delmar's sisters, Deborah L. Jose Tourtillott, and I were talking on the phone, she informed me that years ago, she worked as a Community Health Representative on the reservation, traveling house to house, caring for the sick and the elderly, for over eight years. One day, as Deborah was helping her great uncle, he told her, "I'm going to give you a gift. This story is my gift to you, for you to share." He then told her this meaningful tale.

Deborah mentioned that she can't reveal his name because it is disrespectful to divulge a person's name who gives you a gift. I immediately advised her that she would bring so many smiles to many readers if she would allow me to publish her story, which we named "Bird Dance." I then asked Delmar's other sister, Leona M. Jose Marquez, if she would draw the illustrations so that she can bring visual enjoyment with her detailed artistic talent.

As I was telling my daughter, Jena Avila, about my idea, she reminded me that our dear friend, Kristoff Shelter, is the personal assistant to the incredible Kathy Kidd, C.E.O.

of Best Sellers Guild. I then completed her nine-week on-line course, as Kathy and Kris walked me through this wondrous journey of writing, publishing, and marketing.

Thank you, everyone, for your help and support in making this book possible, especially Deborah and Leona. We hope you enjoy reading "Bird Dance."

****

12

EARLY YEARS

A long time ago, when the Quechan Indian Reservation was filled with mesquite trees and weeds and a lot of brush around, a human couldn't walk around there. You had to be an animal to live in this desert, or you had be a bird to fly above the dense native plants and trees such as the tamaracks, salt cedars, palms, and cactus. The trees and natural grown foliage gave shade and shelter to the animals so they could survive the blistering hot sun because for many months of the year, the average temperature was over 100 degrees.

In the middle of the reservation sat this massive mesquite tree. It was majestic to view. This tree was the oldest on the reservation, and many families of birds lived here because it was cool under its vibrant green leaves that looked like little fans. The bird families enjoyed the abundance of seeds this majestic mesquite tree provided. The bird families had first dibs plucking the green pods from the leaves or anxiously waited for them to change color to yellow as they dried up and dropped to the ground.

In this tree, there lived this one family of birds consisting of the mother, the father, and five baby birdies. This tree was the center of their world. It was their home. The father was very stern with his family and taught his sons how to take very good care of their tan and dark brown feathers. He also made sure that his white ring under his neck was always glistening for his wife. He always wanted his wife to be proud of the husband she chose. The mother bird was beautiful, soft in nature, and lovingly cared for her babies as she

14

gathered them daily with her full array of auburn feathers.

As these baby birds continued to grow, their feathers flourished in size, and they were now able to mimic their parents flying. They practiced day and night, flying out of the tree and falling to the ground, dusting themselves off, flying back up to their nest, and landing back down on the dried leaves. They were then determined to fly to the next golden bush. They would set sail at the mercy of the wind, wobble in the air, hang on a big leaf, before hitting the ground again.

Soon the baby birds were flying from one plant to another, and then from one tree to another. They flew in spurts, and soon they were flying from their home to the end of the reservation. They enjoyed their freedom when they were finally able to fly to the top of their majestic mesquite tree, watching the sun turn orange and burnt reds as it set past the wave of tan-colored mountains. The baby birds soon raced each other to see which bird could fly the fastest to snatch seeds from the plants below.

One evening, as the two brothers were on the treetop watching the turquoise sky darken, the eldest brother asked, "Where is that sun going? Where is the wind taking those white clouds to? If the clouds are moving, then I can move, too! There's got to be more out there than this mesquite tree here. I could see far, and I can now fly further to check it out!"

His younger brother told him, "Don't go too far! This is our home. You have to stay here where we're safe. You might get lost!"

The older bird replied to his brother, "I'm not scared because I have great wings! I'm so curious to find out what is out there, past our home. I have to fly away from this tree to explore what is out there."

Soon the anxious bird said good-bye to his family, eager to fly his young chocolate brown and pale white wings to the unknown. His father wrapped his mature strong wings around his eldest son and told him, "You're a great example for your brothers and sisters to achieve your dreams, but be smart out there, and stay away from the coyotes."

His mother told her baby, "Go and see what you want to see, but always remember where your home is."

TEST YOUR WINGS

This desirous bird started following the sun. He told his family that he would follow the sun as far as it would take him. So he flew west. For many years, this young bird watched as this bright big yellow ball rise in the east and set in the west. He was excited. He waited until the sun was on top of him, and then followed it as it was heading away from the reservation.

As he flew away from home into the scorching desert, he saw scorpions and snakes and other things that were at times hard to see because their khaki skins blended with the desert sand. The scorpions hid in the patchy shadows of the land. This thirsty bird made friends with them, as he stopped there to rest and drink.

He came across a small oasis, which had a little puddle of still water. He knew the water was from a well because it wasn't running water. It was shiny clear, and he could see the reflection of the blue sky in the water. So he drank from it. He then sat under a mint green desert palm tree that shaded him from the blazing sun, and he rested. The tranquil bird then found hot springs near plants and tumble weeds. He then cleaned himself and bathed. He also enjoyed the different flavors of worms and bugs from rose, pink, and lime cactus flowers that were blooming, that he had never tasted before on the reservation.

The eager bird flew further until he got to the end of the hills, where he had seen tawny-shaded mountain lions and goats and rams scaling the rolling mountains. He was surprised how thick the mountain lion's fur was. Their dark and light brown paws were huge. They looked like big cats. They camouflaged with the rocks. The grayish goats were scraggly but agile. They were skinny and fast. The gold-colored rams were strong. They had to be to climb those tall mountains.   They looked like big sheep with spiral horns behind their ears. The eager bird talked to them and made friends with these animals.

The rams informed him that their horns grow like rings in a tree. The older the ram was, the bigger their horns grew and spiraled, just like the older a tree is, the more rings it has in its trunk. The baby rams had little nubs on their heads. The happy bird was then able to distinguish who the elders were in the pack.

His new friends also invited him to stay

awhile in their home, but he thanked them and informed them that he had a plan to follow that fiery sun.

24

The eager bird continued to fly as far as he could see. He kept stopping along the way, visiting the animals, learning from them, and making new friends. He noticed that the barren mountains were now changing to a rich forest. The trees were now taller. The plants were much greener. It was cooler here. There were plenty of soothing running streams of water and brooks.

He came upon a deer and a rabbit playing in a flat grassy meadow. The deer was small with big brown and white spots and very slender. The gray and white rabbit was fluffy and chunky. The deer and rabbit protected each other. They both were fast runners.

The hungry bird made time to eat delicious pine nuts and red and black berries. He sat and relaxed as he watched the slow clear water moving through a small tranquil brook, until in his peripheral vision, he saw this reddish-brown coyote lurking behind a tall tree. The coyote's jagged long fur made this black-eyed, sharp nose predator look like a mutt. The pointed ears and ominous stare gave this tiny bird the creeps. Although it resembled a dog, this cautious bird knew he couldn't be friendly with this animal. He remembered what his father told him about coyotes, to stay away because they will eat him.

The nervous bird soon said good-bye to his new friends, the deer and the rabbit, and anxiously headed to the blue skies and white billowy, puffy clouds.

This eager bird could still see that he could fly further. As he was flying away from the exotic forest, he realized that the intense sun was blinding him with its beaming rays of light. When he flew down from the baby blue skies, he experienced the wonders of an unbelievable sight of the enormous ocean. He watched as the aqua waters moved the pounding waves.   He was in awe how these gigantic sleek rocks joined the vast sea.

He couldn't believe how magnificent this place was. The long white sandy beaches were breathtaking, surrounded by succulent tropical plants and palm trees. He was overwhelmed hearing the crashing loud noise of the waves. The ocean brought a cool breeze to his weathered dry face. Although this powerful ocean was spectacular in beauty, this humble bird knew he had to ask for permission to enter its mighty waters and asked the ocean to keep him safe. He then basked on the sparkling seashore, feeling the soft sand between his toes. This felt nothing like the coarse dirt in the desert.

He saw animals and fish jumping in and out of the rippled waters. He was astonished how they could breathe above the water and underwater. He knew these whales were enormous in size because from far away, they were huge. He couldn't get a visual exactly how large these animals were because he had no place to land near them. He made friends with these black metallic whales and sandy seals. These slimy creatures seemed happy when they were honking loud at each other.

The big white and black pelicans were strange birds to observe with their tenacious beaks and big baskets hanging from their mouths. Their eloquent feathers flared out so graciously. The glossy gray dolphins were fun to watch diving in and out of the serene sea. Their smiles on their faces instantly made you happy also.

Staring at the crestline of the dark seas meeting the orange sun, this elated bird suddenly realized and thought, "I did it! This is as far as I can fly! There is nowhere else I can go because I always need a place to land." So he decided to live by this splendid ocean which he considered was paradise. He made his home by the sea shore, enjoying the beautiful breezes, comfortable climate with an abundance of food, green grass, tropical flowers, fruits, and an assortment of other kinds of birds that he made friends with.

31

He stayed living by the ocean for years until one day he got homesick. He missed his mother and father and sisters and brothers. He missed his good friends that buzzed around that big majestic mesquite tree. It just wasn't the same living in paradise without his family around him. He longed for his relatives to experience all that he had.

It was then that this sad bird decided that he had seen enough of the world. He remembered what his mother had told him before he left, "always remember where your home is." And he thought, "I want to go home now."

FAMILY

The next day, the lonely bird told his friends that lived along the ocean with him, "I'm going to fly back home. I miss my family. It's just not the same without them enjoying all of these pleasures with me."

His friends asked this sad bird, "You're going to leave all of this food and great climate and green pastures and beautiful ocean to fly miles and miles away to go back to the desert?"

The eager bird said, "Yes. I need to see my family and friends."

So the eager bird said good-bye to all of his friends by the ocean, turned around, and he started flying back home. He flew with the glaring sun behind him now, allowing the steady wind to drift him home, knowing that it was awaiting in the horizon. He flew east. He was leaving the baby blue skies above the ocean.

Now this eager bird was excited to fly back home. He flew and then rested, ate, and then flew some more, determined to get home as soon as possible to see his family again.

Along the way home, this eager bird waved to his animal friends, the slim deer and the fast rabbits, when he flew by the forest. He noticed that the baby blue skies were turning to a darker cobalt blue. He waved to the squirrely goats, the statuesque mountain lions, and the powerful rams, as he flew by the perky hilltops. The anxious bird knew he was getting close to his home when he waved to the tricky scorpions and the red and yellow snakes, as he flew into the desert. The skies had now turned to sapphire blue.

When this tired bird finally was home, he flew to the majestic mesquite tree that he knew, where he and his family lived in many years ago. But everything around that tree was different. It seemed to hang low now. It seemed darker and not as lively as when he left. There were no birds in the tree. His mother and father and brothers and sisters were gone. His home seemed sad, and so he was sad, and he didn't know what to do. It looked abandoned with overgrown weeds. There was no place to play or feed. There were fallen broken branches all around it.

He said to himself, "I flew all the way home, and there's no one here. I think I did something wrong. I should have never left. I should have never left home. I must have done something wrong."

The sad bird flew down to the bottom of the tree, onto the ground covered with dry ash brown leaves. He sat there, pulled both his full set of wings over his head and was sobbing uncontrollably. He was crying for his mother, crying for his father, and crying for his brothers and sisters. He wasn't aware that his family was in another tree nearby.

His mother had heard her baby bird as he flew over the tree she was in. Even her oldest son would always be one of her babies. She quickly flew next to her baby son as he was leaning next to the tree in a ball, weeping. All of a sudden, the sobbing bird heard a soft voice ask him, "Why are you crying?"

The surprised bird looked up and saw his mother, as proud as she could be. She was just as beautiful as he had left her. He couldn't believe it at first. He jumped up and cried, "Mother! Oh, my gosh! I missed you so much! I came home, and no one was here! And everything is so different!"

The concerned mother hugged her baby bird and replied, "My fearless son, we'll always be around here because this is our home. We'll always be here for you no matter where you go. This will always be your home that you can come back to."

Soon after, his father flew to their family tree, rapidly but assertively, to greet his son who he missed so much. His aged father, now bald, wrapped his son in his long worn feathers and with his low voice said, "Welcome

38

home, my son. I missed you."

His brothers and sisters noticed all of the commotion and immediately flew around their older brother, and started fluttering their wings all around him, screaming and shouting with joy that he was home. Nearby friends of the bird family also joined in on the celebration.

This happy bird then started to hop. He hopped with one foot, and then he bounced on the tips of his two feet. His mother and father and brothers and sisters watched him leap around with glee. They had never seen this kind of move before and asked him, "What are you doing?"

The happy bird said, "I'm dancing!" He continued hopping and spreading both his wide wings out, spinning around, and squawking, and his family and friends all laughed with delight. And they asked the happy bird, "Why are doing that?"

And the excited bird said, "because I'm happy to see you all. I'm happy I'm home!" His family and friends joined the dancing bird, springing and twirling, flaring their wings, bobbing their heads, and chirping, as they all were telling him, "We're so happy to see you! We're happy you're home!"

CONCLUSION

"And that's how the traditional Bird Dance started. We Bird Dance at gatherings because we're happy when we're home or around our family and friends. We Bird Dance when our loved ones have passed away because we know we're sending them home to be happy with their family again."

...Deborah Leigh Jose Tourtillott

CONTACTS

Ft. Yuma Quechan Tribe
WWW.QUECHANTRIBE.COM
P.O. Box 1899
Yuma, AZ 85364

The "Q" Casino and Hotel
(Located on Quechan Indian Reservation)
525 Algadones Road
Winterhaven, CA 92283

Paradise Casino
(Located on Quechan Indian Reservation)
450 Quechan Drive
Yuma, AZ 85364

Red Moon Ale House
Ramiro Marquez, Jr., Owner
(Son of Leona M. Jose Marquez)
130 South Main Street
Yuma, AZ 85364
WWW.REDMOONALEHOUSE.COM

Spirit Mountain Roasting Company
Tudor Montague, Owner
(Cousin of Leona M. Jose Marquez
and Deborah L. Jose Tourtillott)
WWW.SPIRITMOUNTAINROASTING.COM
info@spiritmountainbrewing.com
P.O. Box 1266
Winterhaven, CA 92283

Deborah L. Jose Tourtillott
(Storyteller)
DEBTURTLE1@YAHOO.COM
P.O. Box 183
Winterhaven, CA 92283

Leona M. Jose Marquez
(Illustrator)
Beadwork, Seamstress, Artist
AZCACTSFLR@YAHOO.COM

Eleanor Flores
(Author)
HPYFYNGERS@AOL.COM
P.O. Box 4834
San Dimas, CA 91773

Kathy Kidd, C.E.O.
(Marketing Genius)
BESTSELLERSGUILD@GMAIL.COM

51320415R00027

Made in the USA
Middletown, DE
01 July 2019